CW00435455

THE SOUTH DOWNS WAY

THE SOUTH DOWNS WAY

Belinda Knox

F

FRANCES LINCOLN LIMITED

PUBLISHERS

To my artistic and inspirational grandmother, Rachel Stainton.

Frances Lincoln Ltd, 4 Torriano Mews,
Torriano Avenue, London NW5 2RZ
www.franceslincoln.com

The South Downs Way

First Frances Lincoln edition: 2008

British Library Cataloguing in Publication data
A catalogue record for this book is available from the British Library.

ISBN: 978-0-7112-2853-5

Printed and bound in Singapore

9 8 7 6 5 4 3 2 1

Many thanks to:

My wonderful partner Simon Spinks, whose feet have walked many miles and whose eyes have shared the glory of the South Downs Way for several months; Benedicte Page who encouraged me; Anna Chamcham for her bright ideas and support; Jenny Huggett who introduced me to the geological depths of the Natural History Museum; Nicola Stewart for her wise words; all my hiking friends; Debal Bagchi for his counsel; Peter Brandon's book *The South Downs*, Peter Anderson and Terry Owen's *The Companion on the South Downs Way* for their inspiration; Paul Millmore's book *The South Downs Way National Trail Guide*, which showed us the path; the valued internet articles on the South Downs Way; my grandmother, mother and father for their encouragement; John Nicoll for having the faith to publish this book and his editor Michael Brunström for bringing it to life.

HALF TITLE: A weathered gatepost marks the passing of time. At White Way the walker crosses from the eastern to the western hemisphere.
TITLE PAGE: The view from south from Winding Bottom shows the downland 'terracettes' from centuries past as well as pylons from more recent times.
RIGHT: This tenacious tree clings elegantly to life in Chanctonbury Ring.

CONTENTS

INTRODUCTION

Where e'er you walk, cool gales shall fan the glade.
Trees where you sit shall crowd into a shade.
Where'er you tread, the blushing flowers shall rise.
And all things flourish where you turn your eyes.
Alexander Pope, *Pastorals*

Nature can be a paradox: at once both cool and refreshing and a tumble of howling gales through the sky. Trees can gather together and sound a chorus of whispers, or just provide shelter from the sun. The leaves can be soft and furry, yet hardy – vulnerable in the spring and wooden tentacles still waving in the autumn. And flowers can be both bold and rather shy when their petals first unfurl to the elements.

Yet, as Alexander Pope suggests, the way we perceive nature is the way it becomes in our mind. My earliest experience of the South Downs Way consisted of downpours, wind and extreme cold – all unexpected in a spring in which there had been little rain during the previous months. After about a hundred yards, a plastic mackintosh (bought as an afterthought, seeing as I had done many walks all around the country before and so far mostly escaped rain) shredded as I walked, and the confetti flew high over the cliffs, much to my partner's amusement and giggles. I had no choice but to resign myself to being temporarily, but totally wet. I was buoyed up by the vistas of velvety green filling the walking horizon with the sea crashing against the shore below, and the transient inconvenience became less important.

Even in the harshest conditions there is beauty and gentleness in the scenery. On the cliffs there is wild sage growing as well as the occasional bluebell in a seemingly unprotected spot.

The larger view can be breathtaking for many reasons: rolling fields as far as the eye can see, apparently drifting into the sea, majestic trees, magical sunsets and spontaneous rainbows. Sometimes it can be hard to believe that this is the south-east of England, the most populated part of the United Kingdom, such is the wonderful work that those who preserve the countryside are engaged in. The Way goes through farms, forest land, access land and often every sign of habitation disappears all the way to the horizon. At other times, as the mist descends and the wind blows, the larger view is only a few inches ahead of your nose. As you trek almost blindly along the path in these challenging conditions, others who tread these tracks regularly suddenly loom in the foreground as they continue their regular 'run'.

The South Downs Way was opened in 1972. It was the first National Trail to be developed as a bridleway as well as a footpath. Starting in Eastbourne, it originally finished in Buriton until, in 1987, the extension to Winchester was approved by the Secretary of State for the Environment, so that the walk gathered some extra miles to reach its century. Remarkably, there are people who cycle it in a day for charity and those who run the Way in twenty-four hours. However, there are other ways of appreciating the countryside: some people take bite-sized chunks to walk or ride along; others march end to end in one odyssey. For those horses and riders who work up a thirst, there are many water points en route and a fantastic array of bed and breakfasts and hotels alongside. And there is one other way – walk your eyes through this book. You can go from the beginning to the end of the map in your own time.

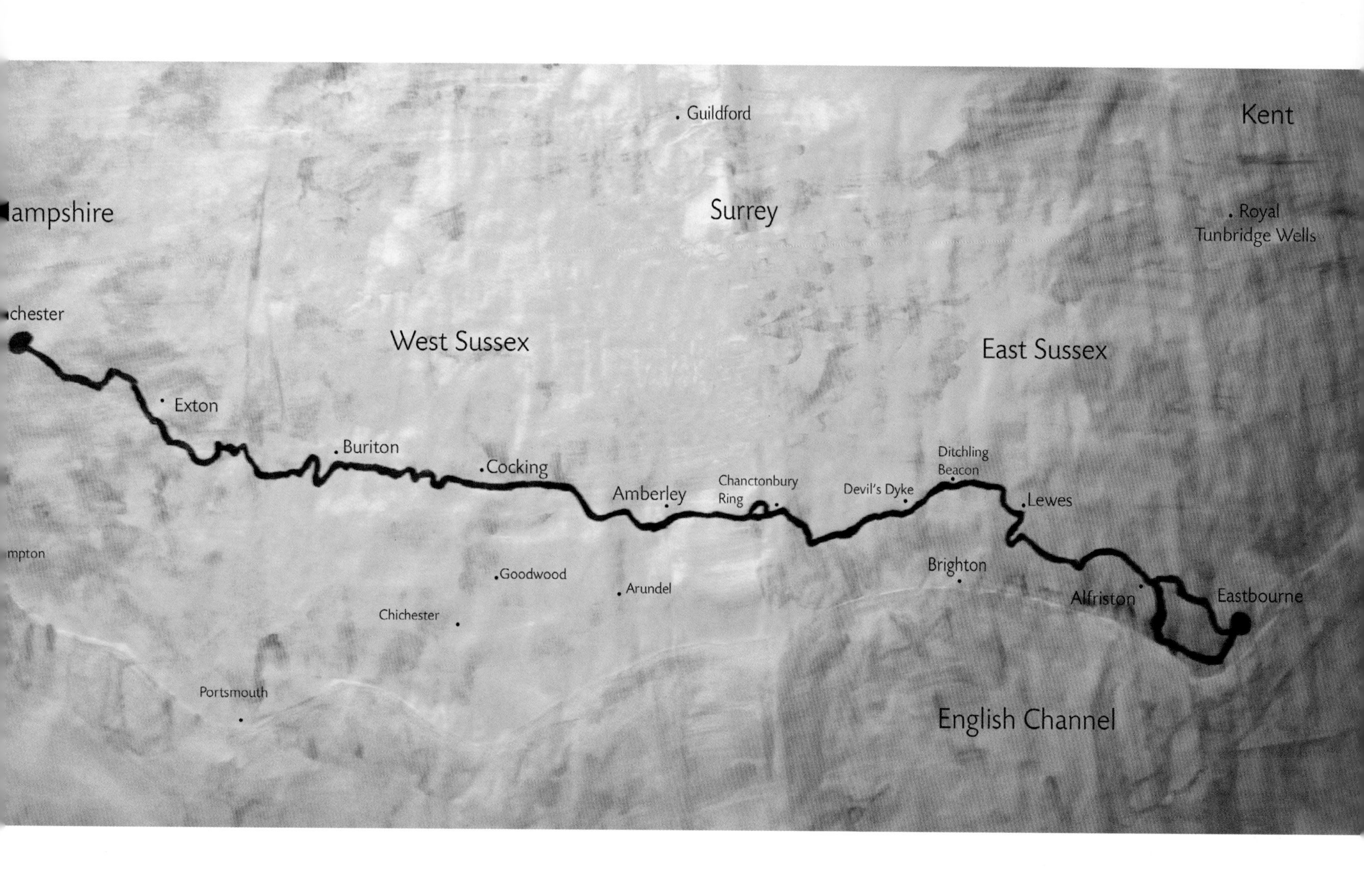
Guildford
Kent
ampshire
Surrey
Royal
Tunbridge Wells
chester
West Sussex
East Sussex
Exton
Buriton
Cocking
Ditchling
Beacon
Amberley
Chanctonbury
Ring
Devil's Dyke
Lewes
mpton
Brighton
Goodwood
Arundel
Alfriston
Eastbourne
Chichester
Portsmouth
English Channel

THE ROUTE

So let us head off along the Way, listing some of the markers that offer a flavour of what you will see in the next pages. The route diverges at the very beginning so that cyclists and riders take the path away from the cliffs, through Jevington to Alfriston, while walkers shadow the Seven Sisters to reach Exceat and a delightful public house before strolling through Friston Forest to Alfriston. Then the two paths converge along the ridge high by Firle Beacon, looking over to Charleston Farmhouse, Firle House, Kingston near Lewes and Lewes, until the route crosses a road by a beautifully crafted bridge to skirt Rodmell. A detour can be made to the village to see Monk's House, home of Virginia Woolf. Past Southease and its wonderful church, the Way continues onwards to Cricketing Bottom. After journeyers move safely over the imaginary meridian line into the Western Hemisphere, their path goes along Juggs Road, up to Balmer Down and towards Ditchling Beacon, with a view of Brighton off to one side. The sea is never far away and it appears as an optical illusion above the track as you head towards the East/West Sussex divide, the Jack and Jill Windmills and Pyecombe.

Nearing Devil's Dyke and Fulking Escarpment the Way becomes very open, punctuated only by the modern world of pylons. At Upper Beeding a cement obelisk offers some sculpture before the path continues onwards past Botolphs, with Bramber and Steyning in the distance and Steyning Bowl close by. Chanctonbury Ring, the Iron Age fort, is now near, and Washington offers an opportunity for another diversion for a pub meal. After a down comes an up, this time ascending to the Chantries. The Chantry Post is an ideal spot for kite-flying

ABOVE: The Keymer signpost denotes the boundary between East and West Sussex. The county of Sussex has been divided since the twelfth century but until 1888 it had a single county council. In 1974, as a result of the Local Government Act 1972, each area was made a ceremonial county with its own Lord Lieutenant.
LEFT: This dramatic piece of artwork is a waymaker that greets travellers crossing over the busy A23 via the Pyecombe Bridge. It was installed by Sustrans, the UK's leading sustainable transport charity. Their vision is a world in which people can choose to travel in ways that benefit their health and the environment: 'Art & the Travelling Landscape' . In partnership with local authorities and others, projects are shaped by local variations and circumstances. Artwork is used to create landmarks, celebrate local characteristics, engage with local communities and make for enjoyable and memorable journeys.

and offers easy access to the Way for families. Once up the steep rise, the Way continues along to Kithurst Hill and Springhead Hill. It reveals wonderful views towards Parham House, Rackham Hill, Amberley Wild Brooks, the castle and village. At this halfway point there is richness of surroundings with Arundel and the remains of Bignor Roman Villa.

From Amberley the path goes upwards towards Crown Tegleaze, down to Cocking, past Goodwood in the distance, before heading into Monkton Wood, over Pen Hill and up to the Beacon.

Continuing onwards comes Harting Down with its adjacent ruined tower and wonderful views towards the village of South Harting. Just a few hundred yards further on the Hampshire boundary is crossed. The Way then goes past Buriton and the Queen Elizabeth Country Park, before the healthy climb up Butser Hill to reach the highest point on the path. Onwards it goes, revealing glimpses of the beautiful village of East Meon *en route* to Old Winchester Hill via a strongly signposted wall and the pretty village of Exton.

The next step is up Beacon Hill, where there are often horses unboxing or boxing up, before the track goes past the medieval village of Lomer, Milburys' public house, Cheesefoot Head and Chilcomb, with a view of Intech in the distance. Winchester is only a few miles away.

Cataloguing the route offers a way of placing the views, which have been taken throughout the year, in a variety of weather conditions. In a moment a butterfly has appeared or a tree, like a dazzling model, suddenly stands out of the surrounding woodland.

ABOVE: The Chantry Post, with all its five limbs in place, is a wonderful spot for kite flying, and as it is beside a car park, offers easy access to the Way for families.
MIDDLE: At the bottom of Beacon Hill on the way to Harting Down, this rather impressive work of art has something more about it than just a signpost.
BELOW: This sign post is on its mettle and here points from Winchester back towards Eastbourne.

GEOLOGY

From what we can see to what we can feel underfoot. The word 'walk' comes from old English 'wealcan', meaning to roll. Rolling suggests a comfortable flowing movement, but the content of the earth that is pounded by foot, wheel and hoof is actually layers of substance. Rocks that form the Downs and Weald are made from sediment laid down in both freshwater lakes and seas many millions of years ago, then raised by earth movements and bent into a huge dome about 125 miles (200 km) long and 50 miles (80 km) wide. As it is soft material it erodes when it is raised above the sea. This natural erosion is still going on today.

The concept of time becomes rather challenging to grasp when you are asked to think back 100 million years. Imagine tiny creatures living in the warm Cretaceous sea. These organisms, called coccoliths, are no more than 20 μm (0.02 mm) in diameter and the platelets into which their shells disintegrate after death are about 1 μm. Other creatures are also present, large enough to be visible with the naked eye, and most of these are either of the oyster family of bivalves or are a type of sea urchin. The fossilization of these tiny animals, which would have created the seabed, continued until sixty-five million years ago. In Sussex this layer has a total thickness of around 300 metres emerging slowly – one foot every 30,000 years. Nature's architecture is beautiful, multifunctional and methodical. In the twenty-first century, where so much is convenience in life, here is an example of creation taking time to kiss completion. During the Cretaceous period, Beachy Head, which is 530 feet (162 m) high, would have been underwater as the sea level was about 700 feet (200 m) higher than it is today.

Subsequently, the sea level fell, ending the deposition of the chalk. Of the younger, sandy deposits that were laid down on pebbly beaches by rivers and by estuaries, very little remains in Sussex. Immediately west of Newhaven you can see a small capping of these resting on the chalk.

Around 30 million years after the end of the Cretaceous, a major period of mountain building resulted in the formation of the Alps. The ripples of this process resulted in the gentle folding of the landscape in south-east England, forming a shallow dome stretching from the Sussex coast to the outer suburbs of London. This was gradually eroded, especially in its central portion where the rocks were soft clays (the Weald). When you look north from the South Downs what you see is the result of this folding and erosion.

Today the porous quality of the chalk holds water, and many of the large conurbations in West and East Sussex derive much of their supplies from this source.

A freshly fractured fragment of downland chalk was mounted on an aluminium stub, gold-coated using a sputter coater and examined in a Philips Field emission scanning electron microscope. This is the extraordinary result. There is a magnification of x5,000, which clearly shows how chalk originated from beautiful shell structures.

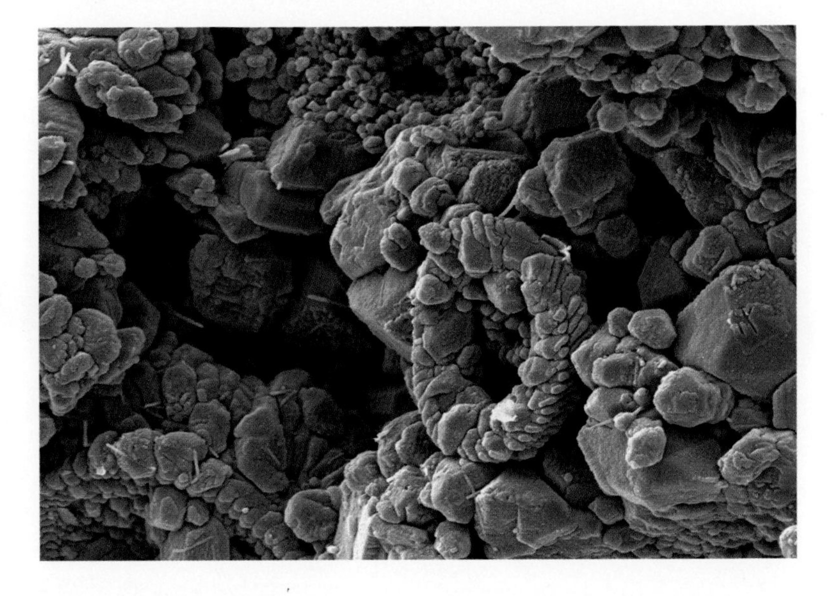

Many years ago, those who looked at this view over Cold Coombes, walking along a part of the Way called Juggs Road, were most likely carrying fish to Lewes market, fresh or salted, in pottery jars on the backs of donkeys.

Another layer is flint, formed by the skeletons of sea sponges into durable seams. It may once have dissolved into liquid as it is often formed into organic shapes and fills spaces in the layers of soil. It creates a hard surface on many of the tracks and also nestles among the chalk.

Flint is still used for cutting primitive tools, knives, arrowheads and axes. The flint mines in Windover Hill, the most abundant at that time in England, may be the reason why there was an early British civilisation in this area. Together with iron, these two substances can be used to create fire. Early inhabitants had a way of keeping warm as well as protecting themselves.

Walking on the Downs it is curious to ponder why they are called Downs and not Ups. The hills are substantial and so the Ups might have been a better description. However, the word 'down' actually comes from the Old English word 'dun', meaning hill. There are several other terms that describe the contours of the landscape: nestling in the clefts of dry valleys are deans, or bottoms, while coombes are the short deep valleys. The Way has one haven: an inlet which affords shelter to ships – or in the case of Cuckmere, used to.

Flint in rock – here we can see some of the flint corridors in the chalk cliffs.

WATER

As has been outlined, rivers cut through the soft chalk while the dome was forming. There are five major waterways dissecting the South Downs Way and one at the end of the path in Winchester. At the start there is the River Cuckmere, which snakes into the sea just by Seven Sisters. When we passed by, a volunteer crew were simulating a dolphin rescue in this haven and taking it back to sea through some of the turns of the water. It was very impressive to watch these enthusiastic volunteers become experts. The plastic 'Flipper' would have had a good chance of survival had it been a reality. The next waterway, the River Ouse, runs past Lewes, crossing the route by Rodmell under a magnificent sleeper bridge. The Adur flows down close to Upper Beeding below a wide metal span and the Arun weaves down to Arundel under the path by Amberley. There is a signpost which shows the place that is equidistant between the two rivers, the Adur and Arun, 12 miles (19 km) apart.

In Hampshire are the River Meon, which runs gracefully by Exton, and then finally in Winchester an ornate bridge rides over the River Itchen. The valleys, such as Devil's Dyke, were either cut by water in a much wetter climate or gouged out during the last Ice Age by permafrost.

LEFT: The River Ouse weaves its way around Lewes downstream to Rodmell and thence to Newhaven.

ABOVE: This is the estuary of the Cuckmere River, a shingle bank guarded by Haven Brow and Seaford Head. It is an example of a meandering river and contains several oxbow lakes formed when a wide bend is cut off by silt. They are called oxbow lakes due to the resulting distinctive curved shape. Some of its history includes details of raiders from France in the fifteenth century and, during the eighteenth century, the haven was a notorious landing place for smugglers. Contraband goods would be brought upstream to Exceat and Alfriston. As recently as 1923 smugglers were caught there with a haul of expensive brandy. It featured heavily in the war effort: at night, lights were placed to confuse bombers into thinking they were above Newhaven and an airfield was set up further inland. In addition to the permanent constructions, the river was heavily mined.

RIGHT: The River Arun flows down towards Arundel. Due to the flood water, the signs on the gate seem somewhat unnecessary. There are three signs – 'Danger of drowning', 'No diving' and 'No unauthorised access'. We hadn't contemplated any of these as we walked towards Bury.

AGRICULTURE, FLORA AND FAUNA

A view from Newtimber Hill towards Poynings and, in the distance, the whispers of Upper Beeding.

The agricultural landscape is ever changing; the livestock seen on the Downs up until the First World War have given way to intensive cereal growing. This has resulted in the ploughing up of the pastures, exposing the thin, sloping calcareous soils to the elements. During periods of heavy rain, with little or no vegetation to stabilise the soil, particles are carried downhill to accumulate in the valley bottoms leaving a predominance of flints. These areas present challenges parallel to those of managing the rainforests. As hedgerows and banks are removed, there is no support to the soil structure, which means that many nutrients can be lost to the rivers. With global warming, the crops will be changing once more and, at the same time, the landscape with transform.

Flowers and herbs have adapted to the chalky layer and the conditions on the South Downs Way. Along the path, not only is there a National Nature Reserve but there are many instances of plants thriving in the most challenging of surroundings. Cowslips, bluebells, orchids and marjoram grow close to the route, oblivious to both strong winds that can blow walkers off course and the hiking boots that may obliterate them in an absent-minded moment. A rather more dainty mover, the butterfly, alights on the leaves of these plants in summer, filling our vision with transient beauty.

It is the traditional sheep grazing on the Downs that has given rise to the characteristic closely cropped turf. The history of the humble sheep goes back a long way. They have been a part of life since biblical times and formed the basis of trade in medieval Britain. Today both wool and lamb are significant, established world trade commodities. There are many different types of sheep often given county or regional names – an example of which is the Southdown, which became the preferred breed in the eighteenth century.

In Britain, sheep farming offers employment, food and clothing for the general population. The droppings also improve the fertility of downland. The practice of shepherds was to allow the animals to roam freely during the day and then 'fold' them –

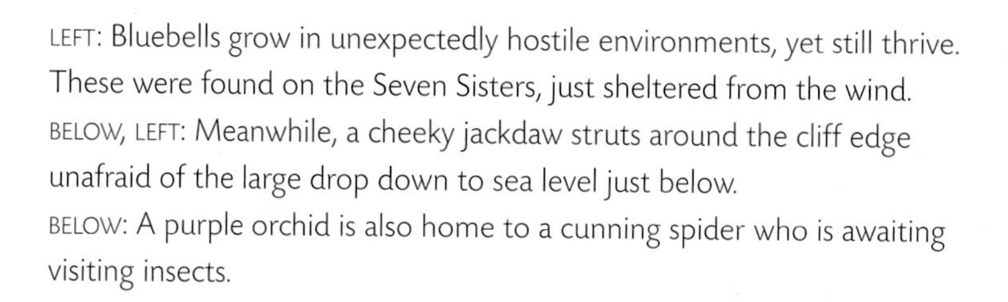

LEFT: Bluebells grow in unexpectedly hostile environments, yet still thrive. These were found on the Seven Sisters, just sheltered from the wind.
BELOW, LEFT: Meanwhile, a cheeky jackdaw struts around the cliff edge unafraid of the large drop down to sea level just below.
BELOW: A purple orchid is also home to a cunning spider who is awaiting visiting insects.

bring them in – at night. The dung collected from their stay would then enrich the soil ready for crops to be planted. There are several downland villages – Fulking, Plumpton and Poynings among them – that developed in this way.

Then there is the comical behaviour of sheep in different weather conditions. In the rain and wind they shelter behind gorse bushes and at the other extreme, in very hot weather they can be found literally pushing themselves into any cover that there may be. While walking the Way I talked to a farmer who told me about basic sheep husbandry. If they are lying down and unable to get up due to the weight of their woolly coat, it can help save their lives by pushing them back into the upright position. When they are on the ground they are vulnerable to foxes, crows and other predators.

The behaviour of cows can be unexpected and sometimes amusing for a walker too. They have been with us for over six thousand years in their domesticated form, providing sources of food for many of us. Human beings have a curiously symbiotic relationship with animals. What differentiates us in the main is our ability to communicate and reflect on life. Cows that have regular positive contact with people will tend to react calmly to walkers.

Along the South Downs Way there are many to meet and greet. As we walked without a dog, the animals did not have to worry about a potential threat. One particular gathering near Chanctonbury Ring seemed very interested in us. Being herd animals they tend to move towards others and have a reluctance to move across contrasting surfaces. They all stopped just short of the track and the cattle grid.

At another time, near Cocking, the cattle gathered at one end of the field for some sort of interaction with us. After admiring these large creatures we continued to walk along the pathway only to hear, a few minutes later, the herd thundering their way to our end of the field to say goodbye.

ABOVE: Hot and bothered sheep lunge for cover in a nearby hawthorn bush in Beddingham. Ouch!
MIDDLE: A long-tailed lamb with its mother near Windover Hill.
BELOW: Curious cows checking us out near Chanctonbury Ring.

SETTLEMENT

Due to its deposits of flint – providing fire – this area of the world became inhabited by nomadic people hunting deer, wild boar, birds and fish between half a million and twelve thousand years ago.

Back in 3000 BC the New Stone Agers (Neolithic) crossed the then narrow sea, now part of the English Channel, and settled on the Downs. The people were semi-nomadic, reflected in their agriculture and trading. As they became more tribal they transformed the landscape by felling many of the trees. There are examples of these settlements along the Way – large enclosures at Combe Hill, which is above Jevington, and Barkhale on Bignor Hill. Other features of life and death at this time were the 200-foot (60-m) long barrows, the communal graves of extended families. As we traverse the Way, our ancestors are literally at our side supporting our journey. A couple of examples are just by Old Winchester Hill and some other later ones on Heyshott Down. Around 2500 BC the burial rituals changed to single graves and there are many round barrows on the high ground. The dip in the middle of these tumuli show that Victorian plunderers had been looking for treasures.

Between Chanctonbury Ring and Washington is an example of a tumulus.

Butser café, built in the style of an Iron Age round house.

By 1000 BC a more advanced civilisation was developing with farmsteads of round buildings and rectangular fields, of which you will see evidence in the following pages. There was trading with Yorkshire for jet, Ireland for gold and Scandinavia for amber, which would have been facilitated by the openness of the route. The population operated mixed farming with cross dykes – farm boundaries – which can be seen by Butser and Pen Hills.

The next great change occurred in around 650 BC, with the advent of iron. As man was able to defend himself more forcefully, the hill forts became more warlike and occupied prime sites. Cissbury Ring is one of the largest of all and can be seen from another, relatively simple one, Chanctonbury Ring. Others, such as Devil's Dyke and Old Winchester Hill are more elaborate. In the Iron Age farming became more organised, as crop rotation and fertilisation were introduced.

Butser Ancient Farm Project has the remit of studying the agricultural and domestic economy of the late Iron Age and it is possible to see how a working farm would have been

Stane Street, the Roman Road built in the first century AD, runs from Chichester to London through both the South and North Downs. It was most likely a trade route for corn and goods from the continent. On the top of Bignor Hill, there is a 'Roman' signpost pointing down to the south to Noviomagus, the Latin name for Chichester and to the North, Bignor and Londinium.

organised in 300 BC. The café on top of the hill offers an example of these old building techniques.

The theme of organisation runs into the Roman era. They saw how important this area of the country was: iron, agriculture and meat were all here in abundance. They ploughed crude fields across the Downs and as a result banks of soil were formed and then subsequent slopes. Each year the bank would grow. These formations are called lynchets. There is a 'waymark' signpost on the route which would wish to suggest that Roman Britain is still alive and well.

A new element in Roman Britain was the luxury home from home. Britain had its own at Bignor, Pulborough and Beddingham, sited on the fertile soul of the Malmstone Bench, and others in Angmering, Fishbourne and Eastbourne.

Let us move on to 477, when the Saxons invaded Sussex. It was one of the first parts of the country to be conquered. The Saxons developed the more fertile valleys and built tracks, or droveways, which can be seen throughout the countryside, for example by Steyning. They may have defeated this area physically but spiritually it was a longer haul before the locals were prepared to embrace Christianity, which means that their churches were built after those in the rest of Saxon Britain. When the Normans came to power they continued building churches so worship became a key part of village life. The population expanded until the onset of the Black Death in 1348 when whole villages disappeared, Exceat being an example. Many local herbs – such as rosemary, sage, thyme and rue – were used in a concoction called four thieves vinegar to ward off the plague and its greatest success was in protecting the doctors and perfumers. (Indeed there is much folklore in Downsmen and women. Marjoram tea was made to cure indigestion and cobwebs were used to staunch the flow of blood and heal open wounds.)

Other factors, such as an extreme drought in 1340 and exhausted soil, contributed to a severely depleted society living in a sparse and diminished way. It was only in the sixteenth century that the Downs came into the modern world. There were two major shifts: feudalism dissolved and the population increased. This led to changes in farming; for example, by the end of the seventeenth century one single sheep range occupied a whole parish instead of many. Proportionally, there was a great deal more arable farming.

In the seventeenth and eighteenth century was a rise in chalk quarrying on the Downs to lime the acid Wealden land and make building mortar. There was also a period of canal building and improved river navigation that facilitated transport on the Arun and the Ouse, allowing the chalk to be moved from the downland quarries to the Weald. Farming in this area became unprofitable in the nineteenth century due to imports of cheaper food from Australia and North America, so much of the land reverted to sheep grazing or was sold to property developers.

At this time, John Ruskin, William Morris, George Macaulay Trevelyan and many other prominent writers and artists were celebrating the countryside as quintessentially English – a source of refuge, an idyllic vision and a spiritual respite. In order to preserve the countryside, the reality of property developers had also to be addressed. The changing life of the countryside was protected by the National Trust and other organisations, who saved parts of the Downs from adverse building. They preserved the Crowlink Estate by the Seven Sisters cliffs. The Duke of York, a supporter of the countryside, came to Brighton in 1928 to dedicate Brighton's Devil's Dyke estate to the public enjoyment for ever. The Eastbourne Corporation bought Beachy Head and many other areas have been similarly purchased for preservation.

On the outbreak of the Second World War, the Downs became an area where soldiers trained and lived. There were many techniques employed to confuse the enemy: disguising well-known landmarks and changing villages to resemble those nearby were two cunning ploys used. Fortunately after the war the lands were returned to their owners and the property development contained. Now the South Downs Way is open for all to appreciate, either in small sections or for others who want to travel the hundred-mile trek, and it offers a journey of spiritual and physical inspiration.

Situated just one mile from the South Downs Way, Bignor Roman Villa has some exceptional mosaics on display, including the longest section in the country and some stunning floor designs. The museum contains many of the objects found on site and offers a commentary.

THE WAY AHEAD

'Do not walk in front of me, I may not follow. Do not walk behind me, I may not lead. Just walk beside me and be my friend.'
Anon.

The Way shows marks of history at every turn and walking it is a wonderful way of absorbing these many facets. While the route has been used for trading, it is now mainly pounded for pleasure and can be a wonderful way to reconnect with nature. For the more meditationally minded among us, this can be an opportunity to experience peace in action as we walk each step mindfully and focussing on 'the now'. A Buddhist practice is to do a walking meditation every day to connect with the peace within and without. All is one. Riding, biking and walking all offer the opportunity to shift easily from our daily routine into one of rhythm, simplicity and beauty. The rider becomes one with the horse, the bike becomes moulded to the person and the ground to the feet of the walker. After several days of this, that is all the mind wants to do and the body follows. Eduardo Galeano summed it up: 'Utopia is on the horizon: I walk two steps, it takes two steps back. I walk ten steps and it is ten steps further away. What is Utopia for? It is for this, for walking.'

This tender scene shows you are never too old to hold hands. Going for a walk is something that people of all ages can enjoy. Whilst children need to be entertained on these outings and made to feel that it is an adventure, at the other end of the scale, those of greater years can find it a wonderful experience as well.

Steeped in history and effortlessly charming, Eastbourne is a gateway to some of England's most picturesque landscapes.

One of the finest examples of Victorian architecture, Eastbourne Pier stretches into the English Channel, allowing visitors to look back at 5 miles (8km) of beach coastline, running from the cosmopolitan marina all the way up to the rolling South Downs.

Eastbourne's floral displays are a major attraction: the Carpet Gardens run along the coastal road near the pier. These flaming hot pokers demand attention as you walk by the pier and they contribute to the awards that Eastbourne regularly wins.

Eastbourne's first bandstand was built in 1893 and six years later a municipal Orchestra was formed. The current building, costing £28,000 and engineered by Leslie Rosevere, was officially opened on 5 August 1935 by Lord Leconfield, Lord Lieutenant of Sussex. The structure is topped with a 24-carat gilded spire and on the wall facing the bandstand is a plaque to John Wesley Woodward, a cellist who went down with the *Titanic* in April 1912. He played in the Grand Hotel Orchestra, the Eastbourne Municipal Orchestra and the Duke of Devonshire's Orchestra.

English seaside resorts would not be the same without beach huts and Eastbourne has some particularly fine examples. These are painted in subtle shades rather than the usual gaudy hues.

Mad Jack Fuller, the eccentric squire of Brightling, built the lighthouse Belle Tout between 1832 and 1834. It was operated until 1902. Many people have since lived here, including a distinguished neurologist, Sir James Purves-Stewart, who subsequently offered it to Eastbourne Borough Council. The BBC briefly owned it in 1986 when it was used as a backdrop to the TV film *The Life and Loves of a She Devil*. In 1999, due to a cliff fall, it was moved a short distance inland. This mammoth task must compare with its original construction when teams of oxen were used to pull heavy Aberdeen granite blocks across the downs from Maidstone. The move to relative safety of just 55 feet (17 m) took two days and in its new position walkers pass around its commanding aspect.

The name Beachy Head derives from the French Beau Chef, meaning beautiful headland. It is the most famous part of the Eastbourne Downland and towers 530 feet (162 m) above the waves, the highest chalk sea cliff in Britain. The wonderful panoramic view extends east to the beaches and town of Eastbourne, the Pier and the Harbour, and then on to Pevensey Bay and Hastings. On an exceptionally clear day, Dungeness in Kent is visible nearly 40 miles (65 km) away. Looking west, you can see up to 70 miles (115 km), past Seaford Head to Newhaven and Brighton and then on to Selsey Bill near Chichester in West Sussex. It is sometimes possible to see the outline of the Isle of Wight.

The Lighthouse, which was built in 1902 from stone and painted black and white, was transformed in 1951 to rings of red and white to assist shipping. Manned until 1983, it is now fully automated. In this picture you will see how the cliffs dominate the lighthouse making it seem small and insignificant by comparison.

These cliffs resemble a gigantic layer cake, and it is clear that nature has a healthy appetite. The cliffs are receding at about 12–16 inches (30–40 cm) each year, and heavy weather precipitates major falls about two or three times a year.

Birling Gap is a beautiful and tranquil enclosed pebble beach set below the dramatic backdrop of the Seven Sisters cliffs. Accessible by wooden steps, the shoreline is also home, just 500 yards away, to a naturist resort.

The Seven Sisters are situated between Eastbourne and Seaford. From east to west they are:

Went Hill Brow, 146 feet (45 m)
Baily's Brow, 194 feet (60 m)
Flagstaff Point, 153 feet (47 m)
Brass Point, 160 feet (50 m)
Rough Brow, 276 feet (67 m)
Short Brow, 214 feet (66 m)
Haven Brow, 253 feet (78 m)

They are thought to have been formed by glacier meltwater at the end of the last Ice Age, which carved steep-sided valleys truncated by sea erosion into the cliffs we see today. The original Seven Sisters are the Pleiades, seven sisters who, according to Greek mythology were transformed into stars. The cliffs have been featured in the film *Harry Potter and the Goblet of Fire* and many TV productions, recently in Channel 4's black comedy series *Green Wing*, in which an ambulance becomes perched perilously on the cliff edge, while the three confused medics inside debate their next move.

Close to the cliffs it becomes very clear how transient this seemingly vast expanse of chalk can be. The soft rock is subject to natural erosion from the sea and the salt and there have been spectacular breakages over the years.

Between Alfriston and Seaford a large white horse on the downs looks east over the River Cuckmere. It was carved in 1924 into Hindover Hill just below the White Way, which also takes its name from the chalk. Three men, John T. Ade, Mr Bovis and Eric Hobbis worked overnight by the light of a full moon and startled the locals in the morning. During the War in 1940 it was camouflaged so that it could not be used as a landmark. East Sussex County Council scoured it in the 1980s and changed the position of the legs from standing to prancing. This helped prevent slippage of the chalk rubble used to fill the figure. The horse and Frog Firle Farm were acquired by the National Trust in 1991. In 1998 the outline was reinforced with timber and chalk.

The Long Man of Wilmington, mysterious guardian of the South Downs, has baffled archaeologists and historians for hundreds of years. Until the nineteenth century the Long Man was only visible in certain light conditions and after a light fall of snow, but in 1874, it was marked out in yellow bricks. There is some dispute among experts about correct positioning of the feet but, despite popular local legend, there is no evidence to suggest that prudish Victorians robbed the giant of his manhood.

In 1925, the site of the Long Man was given to the Sussex Archaeological Trust by the Duke of Devonshire. Similarly to the white horse, it was painted green during the War. In 1969, further restoration took place and the bricks were replaced with pre-cast concrete blocks that are now regularly coated white to keep the Long Man visible from many miles away.

Jevington takes its name from Jeva, who was the chief of a local Neolithic tribe. There was a settlement near the village, and many barrows can be found on the nearby hills. The area was well known for its smugglers. In the 1790s, the most notorious was James Pettit or 'Jevington Jigg', who, as the local innkeeper, would store the contraband in his cellar. While there are no rum runners these days, Jevington is the place for anyone who has a penchant for puddings. 'Ancestral home of the infamous banoffi pie', the Hungry Monk Restaurant displays a blue 'commemorative' plaque on its wall, for the celebrated banana, toffee and coffee pudding. Try the Hungry Monk's renowned recipe:

To serve 8–10:
12 oz (350 g) uncooked shortcrust pastry
2 tins condensed milk (13.5 oz/397 g each)
1.5 lb (675 g) firm bananas
13 fl oz (375 ml) double cream
Half a teaspoon powdered instant coffee
1 dessertspoon caster sugar
A little freshly ground coffee

Preparation
Preheat the oven to gas mark 6 (400°F/200°C). Lightly grease a 10 x 1.5-inch (25 x 4-cm) flan tin. Line this with the pastry thinly rolled out. Prick the base all over with a fork and bake blind until crisp. Allow to cool.

The secret of this delicious pudding lies in the condensed milk.

Immerse the tins unopened in a deep pan of boiling water. Cover and boil for 5 hours making sure that the pan does not boil dry.

(It is absolutely vital to top up the pan of boiling water frequently during the cooking of the cans. Five hours is a long time and if they are allowed to boil dry the cans will explode, causing a grave risk to life, limb and kitchen ceilings.)

Remove the tins from the water and allow to cool completely before opening. Inside you will find the soft toffee filling.

Method
Whip the cream with the instant coffee and sugar until thick and smooth. Now spread the toffee over the base of the flan. Peel and halve the bananas lengthways and lay them on the toffee. Finally spoon or pipe on the cream and lightly sprinkle over the freshly ground coffee. Enjoy!

The fourteenth-century timber framed clergy house near Alfriston was the first building to be acquired by the National Trust back in 1896 for the sum of £10. It bought this virtually derelict property in response to the appeal set up by the then vicar, the Reverend F.W. Beynon. The architect behind the painstaking repair was Alfred Powell, who was renowned as a designer and painter of Wedgwood pottery. This house is an excellent example of early Weald building techniques, including a floor created using crushed chalk and sour milk. Another point of interest is close by: a standing stone enclosed within the stone wall.

'Alfriston' means the farmstead of a Saxon called Aelfric. He received his land from King Alfred the Great in return for military service and is reputedly the place where he burnt the cakes. The fourteenth-century church, dedicated to St Andrew, is built of flint with Greensand corners and facings in a cruciform shape. Often known as the Cathedral of the Downs, it stands in a graveyard within a circular wall. This indicates pre-Christian use and it may have been built on an earlier pagan shrine. Records giving us information on all the rectors and vicars of St Andrew go back to 1272.

Until the 1930s, Alfriston practiced an old funerary custom. Local shepherds were buried holding a small piece of fleece. The idea was that St Peter would have compassion for their lack of attendance at church.

The view stretches gently over the valleys of the Downs. Windover Hill dominates the landscape to the right.

For several decades Charleston Farmhouse was home to the somewhat unconventional Bloomsbury Group of writers and painters, which included Vanessa Bell, Duncan Grant, Maynard Keynes and Clive Bell. Virginia and Leonard Woolf, who initially found the farmhouse, together with E.M. Forster, Lytton Strachey and Roger Fry were frequent visitors. Inspired by Italian fresco painting and the Post-Impressionists, the artists decorated the interiors. The walled garden was redesigned in a style reminiscent of southern Europe, with apple trees, beautiful roses, mosaics, box hedges, gravel pathways and ponds, with a touch of Bloomsbury humour. Vanessa Bell wrote in 1936: 'The house seems full of young people in very high spirits, laughing a great deal at their own jokes, lying about in the garden which is simply a dithering blaze of flowers and butterflies and apples.'

Firle is a compact village nestling at the foot of the Downs. Firle Place, pictured here, was originally built for the Gage family in 1557 but then rebuilt nearly 200 years later around the early Tudor core. The gatehouse of this beautiful house has a miniaturist beauty of its own. East of Firle Place stands the round folly of Firle Tower and around the estate the sheep look lazily at their visitors. Although privately owned, it is open to the public at certain times of year for lunch. The Gage family offered their butler an opportunity to run the catering and he and his wife cook, manage and organise this venture with great aplomb.

Lewes is a rare example of a Norman castle that has two mottes (mounds) with one bailey (wall). When William the Conqueror returned to France in 1067, he made grants of land, including the town of Lewes, to one of his lords, William de Warenne. Within a few years Warenne had built a stronghold here, surrounded by defensive earthworks and a moat. In 1088, William was made Earl of Surrey, and the title continued until 1347, with the death of the last of the line, John de Warenne, the 8th Earl.

Further additions were made in the twelfth century and two semi-octagonal towers were built in the thirteenth century. Later in the fourteenth century a magnificent barbican was added to what had previously been a poorly defended main gate.

ABOVE LEFT: Every year on 5th November, Lewes hosts a colourful parade complete with flaming tar barrels, topical effigies and 'No Popery' banners. There are six Bonfire Societies: Cliffe, Commerical Square, Lewes Borough, Nevill Juvenile, South Street and Waterloo. These tired but happy big – and not so big – chiefs parade back home having been on the 'warpath' in Lewes High Street for most of the evening.
ABOVE: Until the 1870s, the original town clock was housed in the round tower of St Michael in Lewes. In 1881 the timepiece was transferred to the new tower and while the church house was presented to the church, the clock was given to the borough. It was modernised in 1958, when the hand-wound clock was replaced by a new electric mechanism.

The Remembrance Day glow shows not only a figure of Victory above but also Peace and Liberty below. On Bonfire Night, each society lays a wreath at the war memorial and minute's silence is observed amid the drifting smoke to mark those who died for us.

The idea of this crossing was to provide a safer alternative for the walkers, cyclists and horse riders who use the South Downs Way. The scheme was approved by both East Sussex County Council and Lewes District Council, and was drawn up in consultation with local environment groups and affected landowners. The result is a stylish, well-built, functional structure sensitively blending into the countryside's curves.

In 1919 Virginia Woolf and her husband Leonard, leading lights of the literary Bloomsbury Group, bought a modest weatherboarded house in the main street of Rodmell as a retreat from London life. The large garden and beautiful view across the river Ouse to the hills beyond made up for some of the disadvantages of the house. These included a well as the only source of water and oil lamps for lighting. During their years at Monk's House, the Woolfs entertained some of the best-known literary and artistic figures of the day. Among the visitors were Vita Sackville-West, Lytton Strachey, E.M. Forster, Maynard Keynes, T.S. Eliot and Roger Fry. The garden is still as the couple left it. There is a large open lawn where they played bowls, some fine old trees and three ponds. Near the house there is a formal garden where paths, yew hedges and flint walls shelter a herbaceous area.

Just 2 miles (3 km) from Lewes is Glyndebourne, the world famous opera house, opened in 1994, sitting beside the old Tudor manor house. It hosts some of the finest operatic performances in the world. Whilst the main motivation for attending is the music, the experience is considerably heightened by patrons having picnics on the lawn during a long supper break.

Cottages from another age surround St Peter, Southease, which is mentioned in a charter of Saxon King Edgar in 966. The present small building is all that remains of a far larger church destroyed in the fourteenth century. It has an unusual circular westerly Norman tower with a single spire, a nave with a blocked twelfth-century window on the north side, a south porch and a chancel with a blocked south arch. The nave is separated from the chancel by a half-timbered wall with a wide arch.

St Pancras Kingston near Lewes was built in the thirteenth century and has a rare tapsell gate. It is one of six remaining examples of this ingenious way of preventing cattle from entering churchyards while ensuring that coffin bearers are able to pass through without breaking step or shifting their burden. The others are to be found at Coombes, situated midway between Lancing and Bramber, Pyecombe near Brighton, and a cluster of three in the churchyards of Friston, East Dean and Jevington.

The flower of knowledge blossoms alongside this magnificent yucca. Plumpton College was built in 1926 and now offers a wide range of courses on agriculture, horticulture, welding and metalsmithing, animal care and management, forestry and alboriculture, equine studies, viticulture and wine production, sports (outdoor education) and business studies.

Just past Plumpton College, close to a tiny village called Streat, this woodland V was planted to commemorate Queen Victoria's Golden Jubilee in 1887. It has grown substantially since then but retained the overall shape.

High above Ditchling at 813 feet (248 m) the sunsets are extraordinary. Three hundred and sixty degrees of colour in the sky delight the walker: cloud chasers, pink creations and then the sun itself setting. This is the highest point of the walk in East Sussex.

The name Ditchling Beacon refers to the pyres that were burnt here and along the South Downs Way to warn of impending attack, most notably during the time of the Spanish Armada. Rather more recently, they were lit to celebrate the millennium.

The views from this part of the downs are awe-inspiring. See the rolling features of the countryside in this picture, and later the optical illusion of the sea being higher than the path itself.

The story of the two windmills begins in Seven Dials in Brighton where Jill started life. She is a typical weatherboard Sussex post mill built in the nineteenth century. In 1852 Jill was sold to a new owner who organised for her to be towed across the downs on a trolley dragged by horses and oxen to its current site.

Jack replaced an old post mill and was erected in 1866 in Clayton itself. Both ceased to function in 1908 and Jack is now privately owned. The Jack and Jill Mills Preservation Society has totally refurbished Jill, who is usually open to the public on Sundays and on Bank Holidays. In the second picture two of the sails are being painstakingly repaired so that she can pass her regular seven-year check-up.

In the village of Clayton there is a house with a railway right through the middle. There is a wonderful tune sung by Alma Cogan, lyrics by Vaughn Monroe, about a train making its regular journey through the middle of a house and how the occupants' lives go on around it. They live in the front and the back, but 'there ain't no living in the middle of the house, 'cause that's the railroad track!'

Pyecombe Church was built from flint in the Norman era. The tower, with its familiar Sussex cap, is later a thirteenth-century addition. There is a deep cylindrical font of decorated lead which is one of only three in Sussex surviving the Civil War.

To many, hiking seems like a leisurely way to spend a day. However, on one of my first long treks, I discovered that the use of walking sticks helped make it a more enjoyable experience for all the limbs. My footsore companion readily embraced the concept on the South Downs Way and was delighted to find, *en route*, a wonderful craftsman, Dave Bennett, who made and sold them from his house. We purchased an elegant example from his collection.

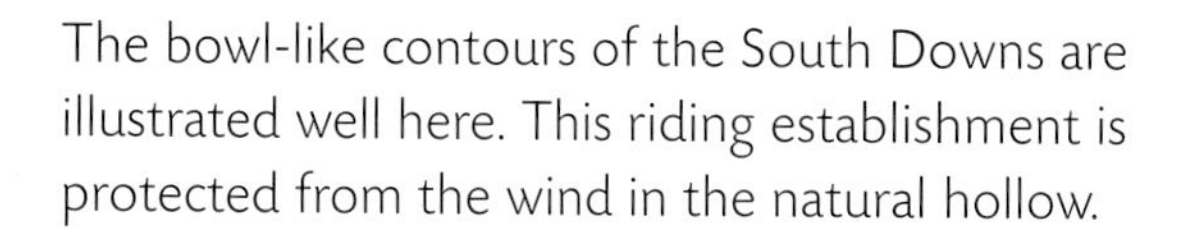

The bowl-like contours of the South Downs are illustrated well here. This riding establishment is protected from the wind in the natural hollow.

The power of the wind! Looking slightly battered, this type of tree is a familiar sight on the Downs. It has two distinct sides – the windblown and the sheltered, hence the misshapen appearance. You can just make out the high rise blocks of Brighton in the distance.

The West Pier, built in 1866, was designed and engineered by Eugenius Birch to attract visitors and survive in the hostile marine environment. It was built using dozens of cast-iron threaded columns screwed into the seabed and strengthened by a network of ties and girders to support a promenade deck. In 1875 a central bandstand was added and in the 1880s weather screens were installed along the full length of the pier, along with landing stages for steamers and a large pier-head pavilion. It has Grade I listing and, although savaged by fire, wind and water and being in the sunset of its reign, it still clings to life.

Although the Way itself skirts around the city, Brighton can be glimpsed for most of the way from Ditchling Beacon to Devil's Dyke. It is a multi-cultural, buzzing, artistic centre which has a large population of students. The Pavilion takes pride of place with its Indian exterior and Chinese interiors, where the dragons of good fortune grace every room. The extravagant building seems at home in a city well known for its bohemianism, Britain's answer to the Taj Mahal.

The Royal Pavilion grew over thirty-five years from a simple farmhouse to a spectacular palace. In 1787 Henry Holland turned the original humble dwelling into a neo-classical building know as the Marine Pavilion. John Nash remodelled it in 1815–23 for George, Prince Regent, later George IV, adding a cast-iron framework to support the now familiar domes and minarets.

The South Downs Way is not only a footpath and a cycle track but also a bridleway. There are horse-friendly bed and breakfasts along the route so trusty steeds will be assured of a good night's rest too.

Among the many delights along the South Downs Way are the cloud formations. Here above Devil's Dyke they seem to bounce across the sky. Covering 183 acres of downland, the colourful name relates to the steep dry valley. It is the largest single coombe anywhere in the chalk karst of Britain and is of considerable interest to geologists, its exact origin being a source of debate. As for the name: local mythology claims that the Devil attempted to carve a dyke through the downs so that the sea could flood the churches of the Weald. Working through the night he shovelled the earth into great mounds, but he was interrupted by a lady with a candle, whom he mistook for dawn.

These distinctive trees border the Tottington Barn Youth Hostel on Truleigh Hill by Upper Beeding. Although close up it looks like a landscaped office block, it is actually a converted summerhouse. Bed, breakfast and evening meals are available. There is also a water point here.

A vast expanse of gentle hills is revealed after a steep walk up from Annington.

A 75-foot (23-m) high section of wall is all that remains of Bramber Castle. It was constructed around AD 1075 for the de Braose family who lived in the fortress for many years. Towards the end of the fifteenth century, Sir Hubert de Hurst and his wife Lady Maud were in residence. Legend has it that the lover of Lady Maud de Hurst, Sir William de Lindfield, was walled up alive by her jealous husband and her ghost visits the castle from time to time. Owned by English Heritage, it is open all year.

Steyning is a Saxon village, which was once a port until the River Adur silted up in the thirteenth century. It became popular with writers and artists alike and included in its midst William Butler Yeats and James Whistler. At Steyning's heart are the timber-framed buildings of Tudor and Stuart tradesmen. Subtle changes over the years have only added to their attraction and the village has 125 listed properties. Saxon Cottage in Church Street, built in 1550, was briefly the museum and it is now owned by the National Trust and can be rented.

Chanctonbury Ring stands 800 feet (240 m) above sea level and can be seen for many miles around. A bronze dagger was found here, along with evidence that a young woman was buried here over 3,500 years ago. A thousand years later a hill fort was built on this prominent spur. The site was abandoned about AD 50 after the Roman invasion, but some three hundred years later a temple was built inside the earthworks. The Atrebates tribe who occupied this area of Britain quickly accepted Roman influence so this temple would have been used by Romans and British alike. In 1588 beacons sited at Chanctonbury Ring were lit to warn of the Spanish Armada.

A circle of beeches was planted in 1760 by Charles Goring of Wiston House. He personally came to the site daily carrying water containers to nourish the trees which, prior to the great storm of 1987, grew in a circle around the mound. Some of the originals still exist and others have been planted so that in the future the circle will once again be complete.

Legend has it that Chanctonbury Hill was created from Satan's labours while digging Devil's Dyke. It was one of the clods of earth thrown up when he attempted to dig a channel through the South Downs to drown the Weald.

Both the remains of a neighbouring hill fort, Cissbury Ring, the second largest in the country, built in 2500 BC, and some Neolithic flint mines, can be seen from the walk looking south.

Dew ponds, or sheep ponds, mist ponds or fog ponds as they have been called, can be found all along the South Downs Way. Early in the twentieth century Edward A. Martin, author of *Dew Ponds: History, Observation and Experiment*, researched their phenomena. He found that the maximum annual dew-fall was a mere 1.5 inches (13.8 cm) – not enough to water thirsty cattle without the addition of an average of 35 inches (89 cm) of rainwater each year. However, from my own research, even during times when there are drought orders in place in the South East, the part of the country reputedly lacking in water resources, the dew ponds are rarely empty. Dew ponds are evocative and much has been written about their poetic beauty and stillness.

Popular from the nineteenth century, they would have been generally made in the spring when the weather is settled, as frost is fatal to a newly-built pond. Clay trampled by cattle becomes watertight and the majority of these structures were lined with clay to which a little quicklime was added to stop worm damage. Some, however, are merely chalk puddles, an example of which can be found in the dewpond near Ditchling Beacon. Yet others had straw mixed with the clay to reduce cracking in the summer and many had a layer of flints to protect the clay from penetration by the feet of animals. Five hundred sheeps' thirst may be quenched daily at such a pond without, under normal conditions, seriously diminishing the supply of water.

Examples can be found high above Alfriston near Firle Beacon, close to Ditchling Beacon and by Chanctonbury Ring.

Just by the South Downs Way track these sheep thought we were the shepherd and his mate and strode purposefully towards us. It was one of those moments of total disbelief on our part, and unfortunate mistaken identity on the part of the sheep.

Looking south-west from this area there are distant views of Arundel Castle, built at the end of the eleventh century by Roger de Montgomery, Earl of Arundel. Subsequently it became the family home of the Dukes of Norfolk and it is still in their remit over 850 years later. Among the famous members of the Howard family are the 2nd Duke of Norfolk (1443–1524), the victor of the battle of Flodden; Lord Howard of Effingham, the Earl of Surrey, who with Sir Francis Drake repelled the Armada in 1588;

and the 3rd Duke of Norfolk (1473–1554), uncle of Anne Boleyn and Catherine Howard, both of whom became wives of King Henry VIII (1491-1547). It has been used in many films, notably *The Madness of King George*.

The castle gatehouse was built around 1080 and the circular keep was possibly begun by Robert de Belleme and finished by Henry I when he took control of the castle. Wild cyclamen grow in the garden below.

Amberley claims to be one of the prettiest villages on the Downs. The thatched cottages, sandstone houses and the village pottery, where items are hand-made in the traditional way, would attest to this. In the Amberley Working Museum there are 36 acres in which you can see a narrow-gauge railway, a vintage bus collection and it is possible to visit many local craftsmen here too. The village is also home to a valuable old post box, still in operation, dating back to Queen Victoria's reign.

Amberley Castle itself is actually a fortified manor house. It abuts the church and stands in land given in 682 to St Wilfrid, who is credited with bringing Christianity to the South Saxons. The house was built in 1100 by Ralph Luffa, the Bishop of Chichester. King Richard II authorised the crenelation in 1377 and Amberley gained its protection. It is now a hotel and not only offers six-star treatment but also boasts black swans, white peacocks and, in each room, a jacuzzi. At the end of the drive, Mistletoe Lodge, a magical thatched tree house reached by a rope bridge and walkway, sits in the bower of a mighty oak.

Bury village here seen from Houghton Hill. The novelist John Galsworthy lived in Bury House from 1926 until his death in 1933. His views were progressive: he supported prison reform, votes for women and opposed censorship. His plays *Strife* (1909) and *Justice* (1910) dealt with the themes of poverty, class and injustice. Amongst a prolific output, he also wrote *The Forsyte Saga* and was awarded the Nobel Prize for Literature in 1932.

Elderberries growing in the wonderfully named Egg Bottom Coppice. There are many opportunities to enjoy the the hedgerow on the walk. Blackberries, sloes, quinces, crab apples and medlars are all waiting to be picked.

Looking westwards towards Houghton. History relates that in 1651 Charles II, then uncrowned, rode by this very spot on his escape from the Roundheads. He managed to live in exile for nine years until he returned for his coronation.

In the distance is Chichester Cathedral, which has been with us since the Chantries. This place of worship is situated in a multi-styled city – primarily Georgian but surrounded by medieval walls and based on Roman foundations. Built on the site of an earlier Saxon church, the current building was started in the early 1100s. It has its own saint, St Richard, who was appointed Bishop of Chichester in 1244 although King Henry III opposed this strongly. As a result there was no money to carry on services. However, the spiritual leader continued with his work until the King finally relented and started giving the parish funds once more.

Crown Tegleaze at 803 feet (253 m) is the highest point on the Sussex Downs. Butser Hill makes up the Hampshire complement at 885 feet (270 m).

The river of rapeseed in Stickingspit Bottom is parted by the Way but grows high enough to envelope all but the tallest of people.

Perhaps the beech tree was tired from sapping seasons, but it was still very elegant in its rather sedentary position.

Catching the two farms in the valley below, this picture shows the Way stretching back to Heyshott Down.

At a branch in the footpath that climbs up Middlefield Lane, stands this large piece of chalk land art created by internationally famous Andy Goldsworthy. This is one of fourteen impressive chalk stone spheres which have been placed around the Sussex Downs.

'The tree which moves some to tears of joy is in the eyes of others only a green thing that stands in the way. Some see Nature all ridicule and deformity, and some scarce see Nature at all. But to the eyes of the man of imagination, Nature is Imagination itself.'
William Blake, *The Letters*

Just above Monkton Houses there are some unusual beech trees. William Blake would have enjoyed these *Fagus sylvatica* 'Aspleniifolia', a rare fern-leaved type.

Sitting on History, Bill Woodrow. This was purchased to celebrate winning the National Art Collections Fund Prize 1996. It was an opportunity for Bill Woodrow to realise one of three ideas for sculptures that could function as seats at Cass Sculpture Park at Goodwood.

Goodwood hosts many races – the horse variety as well as those undertaken on wheels. The royal circuit is rightly famous for its car race meetings and each year it holds the Festival of Speed. Goodwood also hosts special days on which it is possible to drive Minis around the circuit, learn how to corner quickly or get behind the wheel of an E-type Jaguar, Porsche, Aston Martin or an AC Cobra. It has been said that it is because of the Cobra that we have a 70 mph speed limit. Based in Thames Ditton in the 1950s, the cars were raced up the A3 at night to test them. The restriction was introduced in order to curb such enthusiasm.

Some types of mushroom appear growing on the ground in a circle, in what is known as a 'fairy ring'. This happens when the main fungus spreads outwards underneath the soil, like a growing puddle, and mushrooms pop up at the edges. To happen upon a fully formed one was a privilege. Unlike plants, fungi cannot produce their own food. Instead the absorb nutrients from their surroundings. These small fungi are called *Mirasmus oreades*.

This multi-coloured mollusc was sighted after a steep climb up Pen Hill from Philiswood Down. This is a white-lipped snail (*Cepaea hortensis*), rather similar to its brown-lipped cousins but their mobile homes are generally smaller, being only ½–¾ inch (16–20 mm). They have a white instead of brown margin or 'lip' to the mouth of the shell. They feed on grass and low-growing plants at night and after rain.

After the rain stopped and the air cleared, these beech trees started steaming eerily.

This red fungis, fly agaric (*Amanita muscaria*) is inedible and poisonous to humans. Nevertheless it brings a splash of colour to an otherwise green and brown carpet, and it is useful for keeping the population of pests down.

Beacon Hill, which stands at 800 feet (242 m), is an awe-inspring climb. There are concrete remains on this hilltop from a telegraph station. One of a series created in the late 1700s, it gave warning of French invasion. The shutters on the roof could be opened and closed in sequence to pass messages from Portsmouth Docks to London in just fifteen minutes. This system was replaced in 1814 by telegraph lines. The official South Downs Way goes around the hill, which is certainly an easier walk, but the steep climb to its summit has its own rewards. The dramatic landscape of the 100-acre site includes some of the finest remaining chalk grassland and contains nationally important communities of attractive plants such as round-headed rampion, man orchid and field fleawort.

Nestling in an area described as The Bosom, The Vandalian Tower is only a shadow of its former self. It was built for Sir Matthew Featherstonhaugh of Uppark by Henry Keene in 1774. Vandalia is the name of a North American colony and unfortunately, it proved to be a poor investment for Sir Matthew. History relates that his son Harry enjoyed the company of women and used the folly for his private encounters. It has been suggested he had a colourful love life first with illegitimate children and later taking a wife fifty years his junior.

H.G. Wells would have had this tower imprinted on his psyche as his mother was the housekeeper at Uppark. The house appears in *Tono-Bungay* (1909) as Bladesover.

Harting Down is one of the largest areas of ancient chalk downland owned by the National Trust. This local nature reserve and SSSI (Site of Special Scientific Interest) has traditionally been grazed by sheep. It has not been ploughed for many years, evidenced by the small hillocks which are the home to yellow meadow ants. Those areas that were ploughed in the early 1970s are now reverting to pasture. The area is part of the South Downs ESA (Environmentally Sensitive Area).

Is it to East Sussex or to Hampshire that you are heading? This wonderful tree grows close to the border and weathers all directions.

These copper beech trees (*Fagus sylvatica* 'Atropurpurea') sweep majestically around a corner to finish off a curve in the landscape. It is unusual to see so many beeches planted close together but here they are, buffeted by winds, keeping up mass support.

Until 1989 the South Downs Way finished just before Buriton. Now, this picturesque village becomes one more wonderful community visited while traversing the path. It is a delightful place with inhabitants taking a real pride in flora and fauna and their village. They have an extremely active community website and annual fayre in the autumn. The village's insignia is a flying duck, and in this picture a few of them are checking out the bread supplies around the pond.

In 1928 the Forestry Commission acquired Holt and War Down to plant trees for timber, so grazing ceased. When in 1966 Hampshire County Council purchased Butser Hill, this created a combination of downland and woodland and a new partnership was formed. The Queen Elizabeth Country Park was formally opened by Her Majesty the Queen in 1976. It offers recreational opportunities for all. There are sites for barbecues available and beautiful walking through its 1,400 acres of beech and conifer plantations.

Standing at 885 feet (270 m), Butser Hill is a mighty mound. As the walker climbs up, the hidden heights of the hill become more and more evident. It was in regular use throughout prehistory. Neolithic flints and axes have been uncovered at this site, Bronze Age round barrows still survive and there is evidence of Iron Age and Romano-British field systems on the summit. Also at Butser Hill are cows that graze at the top, an old Morris Traveller rests in the car park (see overleaf) and a mock Iron Age round house which offers refreshment during the summer (see page 17). The views show the rolling fields far into the distance.

The sun sets over the two radio masts on Wether Down near the naval base of HMS *Mercury*. The base was active during the Second World War and 500 naval personnel worked here in what was the Navy's main signal school for communications and electronic warfare.

The views into the valley espy East Meon, a picturesque village. This thatched cottage shone through the almost tropical rain shower that had just drenched everyone in the vicinity.

Set up by the Earthworks Trust, The Sustainability Centre has 55 acres of woodland and natural chalk downland and has a mission to 'demonstrate, develop and promote knowledge, skills, technologies and lifestyles that improve people's quality of life without damaging the local and global environment'. There are courses that range from permaculture to mosaic making and medieval roofing. Also, here, they run the South Downs Natural Burial Site, managed on ecologically sound lines to offer both a resting place for those who have died and a peaceful haven for reflection.

A bench to celebrate The Life of Bryan brings a wry smile to a walker's face. Sitting on this bench dedicated to a local man one cannot help but look on the bright side of life.

The valley stretches out into the distance
sectioned neatly by trees planted across the view.

The River Meon flows under the A32 and down through Exton.

By the side of the road, there stands a neat, tidy hornbeam (*Carpinus fastigiata*).

Exton village dates back to AD 940 and the place of worship, St Peter and St Paul, was built as an Early English two-cell church in the twelfth century. It is built of flint and mortar and has an unusual 'weeping chancel' with a distinct angle at the junction with the nave.

Of particular interest is a beautifully elegant, stencilled painting on the east wall behind the altar. Designed by Charles Spooner in the 1890s at the same time as he created the stained glass windows, it offers a stylized, almost pagan-influenced 'Tree of Life'. It is fortunate that we can view this masterpiece as it was covered up in the mid 1920s as a result of damp and only rediscovered in 1995 by chance. The inscription reads: 'O all ye works of the Lord, bless ye the Lord, Praise him and magnify him for ever.'

Down the road in Exton there is a wonderful pub called The Shoe. One of the great London cobblers donated this size 24 brogue that sits so proudly on their mantelpiece. Several other cabinets reflect the theme with delightful examples of other, rather smaller, footwear. The food here is wonderful and worth a few visits to get through the menu.

Come rain or shine, this stile faithfully moves walkers from one field to another.

High on the Beacon there is plentiful flora including this silverweed, which seems to shine in the sun.

The gentle view in this field between Beacon Hill and Preshaw Down stretches towards Exton.

There was a Saxon estate and an early medieval village of Lomer, which was occupied from the tenth century until 1851. Now Lomer Pond is one of the only remaining traces.

The joy of a rainbow is its transience. After a heavy hailstorm, this beautiful cascade of colour appeared over Kilmeston Down.

How this beech tree has transformed! Whilst its colours have changed, the overall shape holds fast – from green to gold as the seasons unfold.

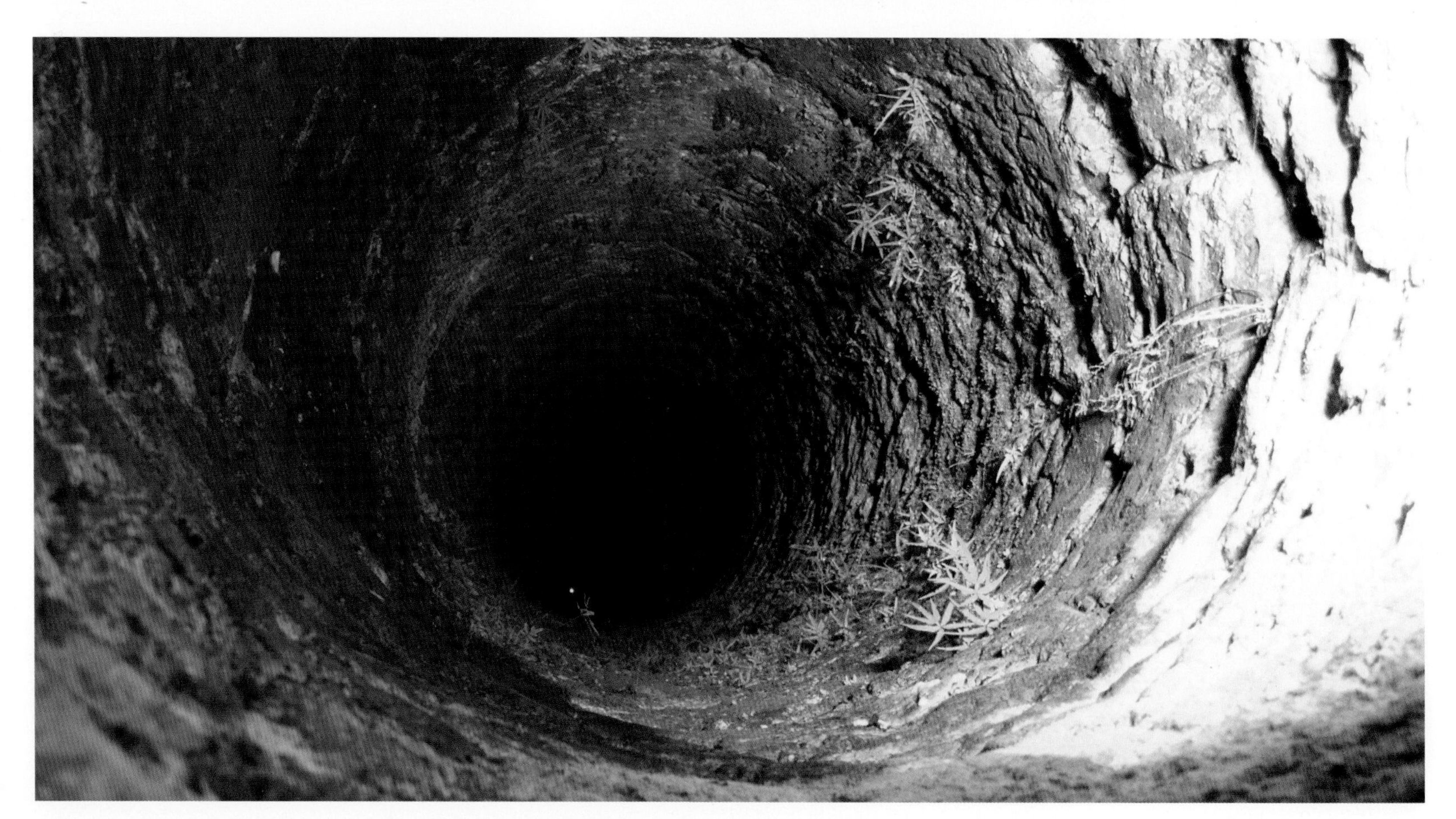

There is more than one way to make it to Milburys. A horse and trap or a classic Jaguar both appeared with their owners for lunch at this pub/restaurant where there is a 300-foot (90-m) well. Covered by a metal casing, the bottom is just visible to the naked eye and ice cubes can be purchased to drop into the depths below.

On May Day Bank Holiday, there is a festival held in the Devil's Punchbowl, where several tents offer musical entertainment. To a passing walker's ear, the cacophony of sound makes any one offering totally indistinguishable. However, there were throngs of people enjoying the celebrations. History has it that in 1944 General Eisenhower addressed the allied troops here before the D-Day landings on June 6, 1944.

While the hustle and bustle of city life has all but left red telephone boxes redundant in favour of the mobile, here in a country garden one finds a loving retirement home.

The sweeping views look up to Cheesefoot Head from the quiet village of Chilcomb.

Possibly a UFO but in reality INTECH, an educational charity run by the Hampshire Technology Centre Trust Ltd. This centre is open every day between 10am and 4pm. Here there is the chance to create your own tornado and understand how to bend light . . . perhaps enough for one day out. As a family science centre, it helps bring the world of science and technology to life.

Almost bowing out of respect for their physical efforts, these houses welcome weary travellers at the end of the South Downs Way into Winchester.

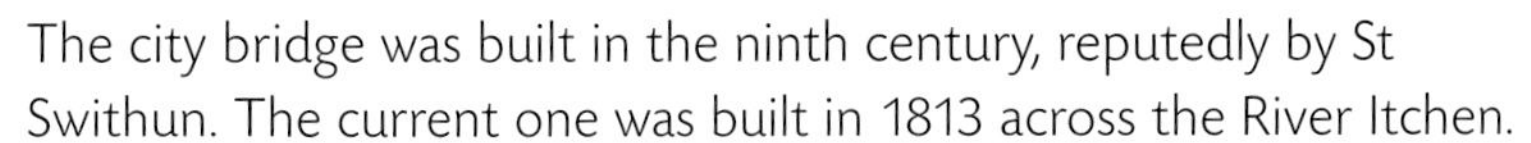

The city bridge was built in the ninth century, reputedly by St Swithun. The current one was built in 1813 across the River Itchen.

When the Romans arrived they created a walled city which they called Venta Belgarum. Later in AD 871 King Alfred was crowned and he made the city of Winchester the capital of Saxon England. This statue of the monarch with his sword ready for battle was sculpted by Hamo Thornycroft and was placed on the Broadway in 1901.

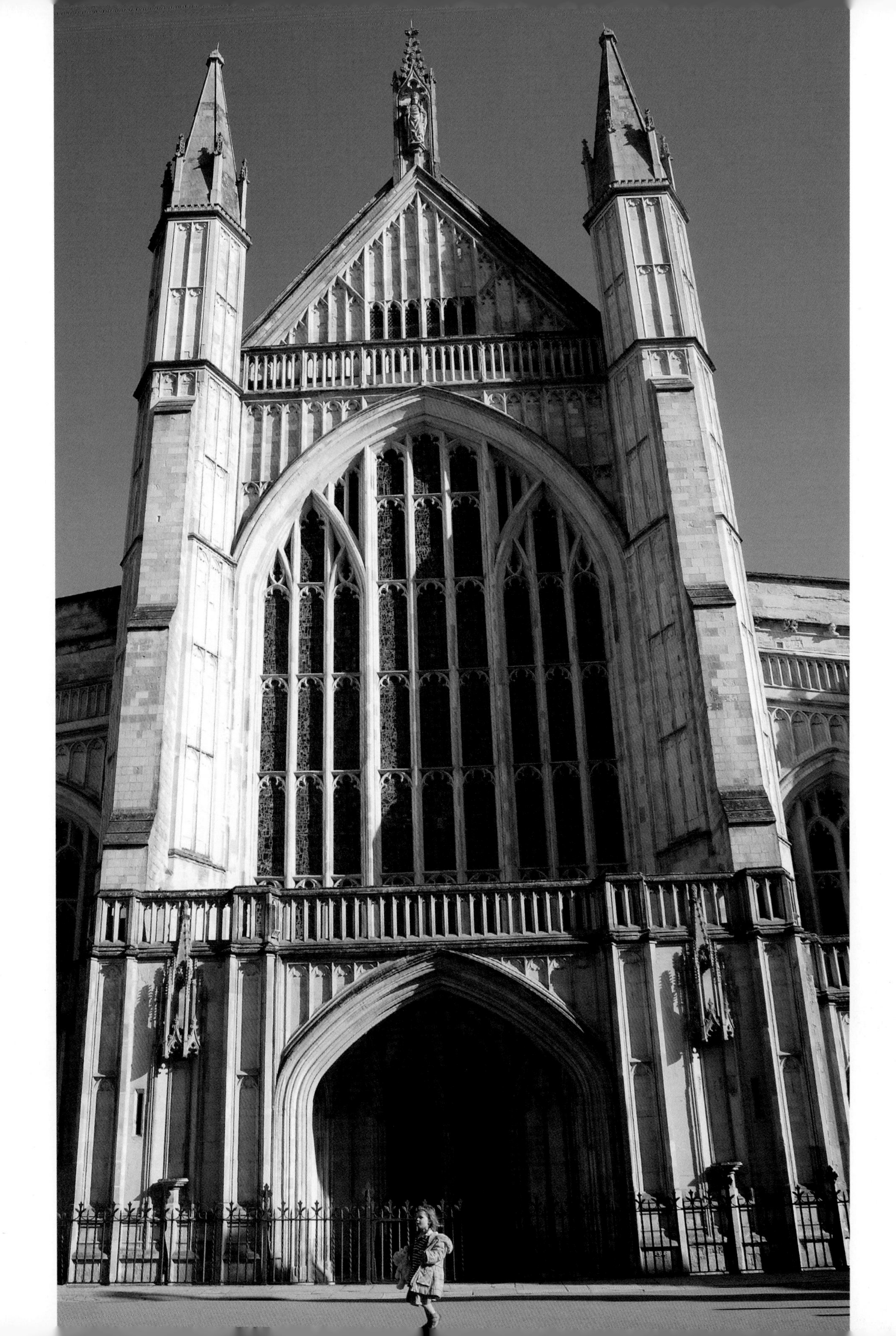

The Cathedral dates back to 1079, when William the Conqueror commenced building work. Due to one extremely loyal man, William Walker, it still stands today. The foundations were originally laid on peat and, in order to rectify chronic subsidence, he was employed for six years between 1906 and 1912 to replace the rotting vegetation with concrete. William had to wear full diving gear and work in 3.5 metres of ground water. There is a statue in the cathedral to honour his efforts.

This fig tree climbs around the restaurant area of the cathedral.

At the Giffard House Hotel, almost anything is possible. The comfortable beds and scenic bedrooms are welcome after a hundred miles of walking. At breakfast Mrs Bridges the parrot has a few words to say to visitors. 'Hello,' is her first gambit and if you really get into conversation with her she asks you how are you doing. If I were Mrs Bridges I would ask you whether you have enjoyed this pictorial gaze along the South Downs Way. I very much hope you have.

INDEX